W9-AYO-743

Primary Sources of the Civil Rights Movement

Coretta Scott King and the Center for Nonviolent Social Change

Jackie F. Stanmyre

Cavendish
Square

New York

Published in 2017 by Cavendish Square Publishing, LLC
243 5th Avenue, Suite 136, New York, NY 10016

Library of Congress Cataloging-in-Publication Data

Names: Stanmyre, Jackie F., author.
Title: Coretta Scott King and the Center for Nonviolent Social Change / Jackie F. Stanmyre.
Description: New York : Cavendish Square Publishing, [2016] | Series: Primary sources of the civil rights movement | Includes bibliographical references and index.
Identifiers: LCCN 2016006895 (print) | LCCN 2016012679 (ebook) | ISBN 9781502618764 (library bound) | ISBN 9781502618771 (ebook)
Subjects: LCSH: King, Coretta Scott, 1927-2006. | African American women civil rights workers--Biography--Juvenile literature. | Civil rights workers--United States--Biography--Juvenile literature. | Martin Luther King, Jr. Center for Nonviolent Social Change--Juvenile literature. | King, Martin Luther, Jr., 1929-1968--Juvenile literature. | African Americans--Civil rights--History--20th century--Juvenile literature. | Civil rights movements--United States--History--20th century--Juvenile literature. | African Americans--Biography--Juvenile literature.
Classification: LCC E185.97.K47 S73 2016 (print) | LCC E185.97.K47 (ebook) | DDC 323.092--dc23
LC record available at http://lccn.loc.gov/2016006895

Editorial Director: David McNamara
Editor: Fletcher Doyle
Copy Editor: Nathan Heidelberger
Art Director: Jeffrey Talbot
Designer: Amy Greenan
Production Assistant: Karol Szymczuk
Photo Research: J8 Media

The photographs in this book are used by permission and through the courtesy of:
Jean-Claude Francolon/Gamma-Rapho/Getty Images, cover; Library of Congress, 5, 6; AP Photo/Butch Dill, 8; Ed Clark/The LIFE Picture Collection/Getty Images, 10; New York World-Telegram and the Sun staff photographer: Al Ravenna/Library of Congress/File: NAACP leaders with poster NYWTS.jpg/Wikimedia Commons, 12; Seth Poppel/Yearbook Library, 13; Don Cravens/The LIFE Images Collection/Getty Images, 16; Don Cravens/The LIFE Images Collection/Getty Images, 18; AP Photo, 19, 31; AP Photo/Eddie Adams, 21; AFP/AFP/Getty Images, 22; AP Photo/David Longstreath, 23; CBS Photo Archive/Getty Images, 24; Raymond Boyd/Getty Images, 26-27; Lee Balterman/The LIFE Picture Collection/Getty Images, 33; ullstein bild/ullstein bild via Getty Images, 34; Diana Walker/Time Life Pictures/Getty Images, 37; David Fenton/Getty Images, 39; Matt McClain/Getty Images, 41; PAUL J.RICHARDS/AFP/Getty Images, 44; AP Photo/Jim Rogash, 45; Joseph Sohm/Shutterstock.com, 47; Gerry Boughan/Getty Images, 48; Dick Swanson/The LIFE Images Collection/Getty Images, 50; Stephen Morton/Getty Images, 51.

Printed in the United States of America

CONTENTS

Carrying
the Message

President Abraham Lincoln signed the Emancipation Proclamation on January 1, 1863. This marked the beginning of the end of slavery in America. President Lincoln said, "I do order and declare that all persons held as slaves within said designated States, and parts of States, are, and henceforward shall be free." At the time, this only applied to certain states. But after the Union (North) beat the Confederacy (South) in the Civil War, everyone was meant to be free. On December 18, 1865, the Thirteenth Amendment to the Constitution declared "Neither slavery nor involuntary servitude, except as a punishment for crime whereof the party shall have been duly convicted, shall exist within the United States, or any place subject to their jurisdiction." In other words: slavery was over.

However, ending slavery did not guarantee blacks would be treated fairly. They were free but still very poor and lived in bad conditions. Blacks were not allowed to attend the same

Coretta Scott King and the Center for Nonviolent Social Change

schools or churches as whites. They also were not allowed to vote. Certain groups began to terrorize black Americans. The Ku Klux Klan terrorized people while wearing their white hoods and **lynched** blacks or anyone who supported them.

President Abraham Lincoln ended slavery in the Confederacy by signing the Emancipation Proclamation.

For black people, this sure didn't feel like freedom. They began a movement in the 1930s. Black Americans wanted to end the enforced separation of racial groups and racial discrimination. They were tired of being treated as **inferior**. They felt they had the right to eat in any restaurant or sit in any bus seat or train seat that they chose to. They wanted their children to have the same access to a good education as the children of white parents. This movement, which came to be known as the civil rights movement, had many leaders. The most notable person was Martin Luther King Jr., a minister and activist known for preaching a message of nonviolence. He believed black Americans should fight for their rights—but with their words and passion, not with their firsts or with weapons.

In April 1968, Dr. King was in Memphis, Tennessee, to support black sanitation employees who were on strike for higher wages and better treatment. On April 3, Dr. King gave a speech titled "I've Been to the Mountaintop." In his speech, he said:

Coretta Scott King (*right*) supported her husband, Martin Luther King Jr. (*left*), throughout his work in the civil rights movement.

We've got some difficult days ahead. But it doesn't matter with me now. Because I've been to the mountaintop. And I don't mind. Like anybody, I would like to live a long life. Longevity has its place. But I'm not concerned about that now. I just want to do God's will. And He's allowed me to go up to the mountain. And I've looked over. And I've seen the promised land. I may not get there with you. But I want you to know tonight, that we, as a people, will get to the promised land.

The next day, Dr. King was assassinated on the balcony outside his hotel room.

The civil rights movement was strongly under way by the time Dr. King died. His message of nonviolence was an important one for the community. But who would make sure that message was carried out? His wife, Coretta Scott King, was ready for the task.

Coretta Scott King and the Center for Nonviolent Social Change

CHAPTER ONE

Meeting Discrimination

Coretta Scott King never experienced life as a slave, but the circumstances in which she grew up were anything but luxurious. Coretta was born on a farm in a small town in Alabama on April 27, 1927, two years before the Great Depression began. Her parents, Obadiah "Obie" Scott and Bernice Murray Scott, worked to make a better life for their children. Coretta was the middle child; she had an older sister named Edythe and a younger brother named Obie.

Coretta's childhood home had just two rooms: a kitchen and a bedroom. The space had to be shared with her parents and two siblings. The floors were bare wood, and paper peeled off the walls. Their wood-frame farmhouse did not have running water. It was heated by a wood-burning stove. The family did, however, have a farm on which to raise animals and grow vegetables. Before school every morning, Coretta and her siblings hoed weeds, picked vegetables, gathered eggs from under the chickens, and fed the hogs.

When her chores were done, Coretta would play with her siblings and friends, running, climbing, and sometimes getting into fights. In the evening, her mother read stories. The family also was known to listen and sing along to blues, jazz, and gospel records.

A memorial service for Coretta Scott King was held at Mount Tabor AME Zion Church in Perry County, Alabama, where she grew up.

Coretta's family was tight-knit, and in speeches she gave over the years it was clear how much she respected her parents. It was through her parents' experience that she was initially exposed to racism. And this is where her anger against discrimination began.

Obadiah Scott was a hard-working man who looked for extra opportunities to provide for his family. He was employed by a sawmill and used his own truck to haul logs in order to make extra money. He worked alongside white men, but they did not see Coretta's father as an equal. The white men thought they deserved the extra work and extra money, and they went to great lengths to try to keep him down. Obie Scott was threatened by his coworkers, who said they would report him to the police as a reckless driver. Over many years, Obie saved enough money to buy his own sawmill. One white man offered to buy it from Obie, but he refused. Coretta remembered that being an issue. She wrote in her book, *My Life with Martin Luther King Jr.*:

Coretta Scott King and the Center for Nonviolent Social Change

The logger who worked in the mill was white, and after my father had owned the mill for about two weeks, the logger came to him and said he wanted to buy it. My father said, "No, I don't want to sell." … The next Monday when my father went to his sawmill in the woods, he found only ashes … My father is such an amazing person. He never became bitter, despite all these incidents, all the humiliations and harassments by the whites who wanted to keep him down because they saw their own jobs imperiled, and because they did not want any black man to rise above "his place."

Coretta's mother, Bernice, saw her daughter's anger growing. Bernice preached to her daughter about rising above such incidents, not getting violent. "You get an education and try to be somebody," Bernice told Coretta. "Then you won't have to be kicked around by anybody." This sentiment of nonviolence stuck with Coretta. However, the school system was as unfair as anyplace else.

Lessons at School

The facilities in all schools then were ordinary compared to the advanced equipment available to students today. There weren't, of course, any computers in classrooms, and many schools used one room to teach several grades. However, the white children had access to better resources. In Coretta's case, the white children in her area also had more convenient accommodations. While Coretta and her sister and brother had to walk 3 miles (4.8 kilometers) to school in Heiberger, the white children in her town took a bus to more modern schools in Marion. Coretta remembered her school as "an unpainted frame building with one big room in which one hundred or more children were taught in the first through

Schools for black children were often overcrowded and lacked resources. These students are sharing scarce books in a school in a Baptist church.

sixth grades … Sections of the wall were painted black, and these served as blackboards. The toilets were outdoors, and the room was heated by the usual wood-burning stove." Two dedicated black women taught all those students in the joint classroom. Teachers did not have to be very qualified to teach black students. They only needed to pass a certification exam.

White children received textbooks for free, but the black students did not. In order to have money for school books, Coretta worked after school and on the weekends picking

Coretta Scott King and the Center for Nonviolent Social Change

cotton. With her mother's message in mind, Coretta finished at the top of her class. There was no high school in Coretta's town of Heiberger. There was one in Marion, but it was 10 miles (16 km) away—too far to walk—so Coretta and her sister moved in with a black family near the high school. They had to pay board to live there, which meant more hours picking cotton to earn money.

When Coretta was fifteen, she and Edythe received a terrible phone call from their parents. The family house had burned down, and the fire department didn't even care to investigate the cause. "No one cared about what happened to black people," Coretta said. Her frustration with the discrimination only grew.

After graduating from high school, Coretta attended Antioch College in Ohio. Her sister Edythe had started there the year before. Coretta quickly realized that her education hadn't truly prepared her for the rigors of a college curriculum. Fortunately, Edythe helped her along.

Once Coretta got her feet on the ground academically, she realized that not everyone was meant to be a pioneer in race relations. Even among the blacks with whom she associated, not everyone had the same passion to do something, despite all their frustration. Coretta decided she wouldn't fight against inequality only for herself, but for all the other blacks throughout the United States who had been denied equal treatment just as she had.

Getting Active

Before completing her degree in education, Coretta joined the college's Race Relations and Civil Liberties Committee. She also became active in the local branch of the National Association for the Advancement of Colored People (NAACP). The NAACP was founded in 1909. Initially, the organization wanted to combat violence against blacks, specifically lynching. From the beginning and still today,

Henry L. Moon, Roy Wilkins, Herbert Hill, and Thurgood Marshall of the NAACP hold a recruiting poster for that organization in 1956.

the NAACP has crusaded for civil rights for all people. The organization has won many victories in the legal system.

In 1951, Coretta graduated from Antioch, but she was saddened by the prospect of teaching only in segregated schools. She began pursuing a career in music, studying voice and violin at the New England Conservatory of Music. Coretta was known for being career focused and not making time for a serious boyfriend. That changed in January of 1952.

Through a mutual friend, Coretta was introduced to Martin Luther King Jr., a Baptist minister working toward a PhD in **theology** and philosophy. The two hit it off immediately. King told Coretta on their first date: "You have everything I have ever wanted in a wife ... character, intelligence, personality, and beauty. I want to see you again.

Coretta Scott King and the Center for Nonviolent Social Change

At most functions during her college years, Coretta Scott King was often the only black person present.

No Help from Above

Coretta Scott had always loved music, but she saw more of a future in education. So in addition to studying voice, she pursued a degree in music education. This required Coretta to spend a year student teaching in an Ohio public school. However, the Yellow Springs School Board refused to hire her. In *My Life With Martin Luther King Jr.*, she recalled receiving no support from Antioch's administration:

> The supervisor of practice teaching at Antioch would not allow me to push the matter when I was turned down. She was the type who openly said, "God did not intend the races to mix." The Yellow Springs schools were integrated, but the faculty was white …
> I appealed to the president of Antioch. He was quite new to the school and no pioneer in race relations. After I told him my story, all he said was, "Well, Corrie, what do you want us to do about it?" … "You might appeal to the school board," I suggested. But, on the teaching supervisor's advice, he refused to act.

Can I?" Coretta was impressed by Martin's sense of right and wrong, and how he thought to approach the inequalities of the world with nonviolence.

Change of Plans

Coretta knew that choosing to marry King would mean something of an end to her own professional dreams. Martin wanted a wife who would put family first. Coretta chose love over her singing career, and the two were married on June 18, 1953. She continued her schooling but switched her major from voice to music education, thinking she would be able to give voice lessons wherever Martin's career took their family. She desired for them to live in the North, where race relations were better. But King felt he could do more good in the South. Ultimately, he took a job as pastor at the Dexter Avenue Baptist Church in Montgomery, Alabama.

Coretta and Martin remained active in the NAACP during a time when landmark decisions were being made. In 1954, the Supreme Court made a major decision regarding the segregation of education that Coretta was so bothered by during her childhood. In *Brown v. Board of Education of Topeka*, Kansas, the justices determined that schooling could not be equal if it was separate. In his opinion, chief justice Earl Warren wrote:

> Segregation of white and colored children in public schools has a detrimental effect upon the colored children. The impact is greater when it has the sanction of the law, for the policy of separating the races is usually interpreted as denoting the inferiority of the Negro group. A sense of inferiority affects the motivation of a child to learn. Segregation with the sanction of law, therefore, has a tendency to [retard] the educational and mental development of Negro children and to deprive them of some

Coretta Scott King and the Center for Nonviolent Social Change

of the benefits they would receive in a racial[ly] integrated school system.

… We conclude that, in the field of public education, the doctrine of "separate but equal" has no place. Separate educational facilities are inherently unequal. Therefore, we hold that the plaintiffs and others similarly situated for whom the actions have been brought are, by reason of the segregation complained of, deprived of the equal protection of the laws guaranteed by the Fourteenth Amendment.

While more work was to be done with the civil rights movement, Coretta's primary role shifted that next fall. On November 17, 1955, Coretta gave birth to the couple's first child, Yolanda Denise King, who was nicknamed "Yoki." Three more children followed over the next nine years: Martin III, Dexter, and Bernice.

Despite being a mother first, Coretta worked hard to support her husband's efforts in the fight for civil rights. Just two weeks after Yoki was born, on December 1, Rosa Parks refused to give up her bus seat to a white man in Montgomery, Alabama, as required by the laws of that city. She was arrested, tried on December 5, and fined $14. While Coretta was home with their newborn, Martin Luther King Jr. was helping to organize the Montgomery bus boycott. The boycott began the day Parks went on trial. The *Crusader*, the NAACP's newspaper, wrote about the decision to continue the boycott after its first successful day:

In protest against the fine of a Negro woman for refusing to go to the rear of a city bus here, Negroes all but stopped using that mode of transportation. It was estimated that the Montgomery City Bus Line has experienced an 85 per cent drop in Negro patronage.

At a mass meeting held last Monday [December 5], some 5,000 voiced approval of the boycott and passed a resolution to continue it until bus patrons are no longer "intimidated, embarrassed and coerced."

Martin offered his church as a place for Montgomery ministers and civic leaders to meet. Both he and Coretta knew this put their family at risk. Two months after the boycott started, someone threw a bomb onto the Kings' front porch. No one was hurt, but the living room was filled with glass and there was a hole in the concrete floor. Still, Coretta didn't flinch in her support to Martin and the civil rights movement.

Martin Luther King Jr. gets ready to board a bus in Montgomery, Alabama, after the successful conclusion of the bus boycott.

Coretta Scott King and the Center for Nonviolent Social Change

CHAPTER TWO

Filling Many Roles

Martin Luther King Jr. made it clear to his wife that he thought her number one priority must be the protection and support of their family. Coretta accepted this for the most part. Martin was arrested thirty times and sometimes jailed for peacefully protesting racial inequalities. This left Coretta at home with the children, trying to shield them from the violence or backlash. Still, Coretta remained involved and had an important presence in the civil rights movement from the beginning.

Coretta joined with her husband as they organized students in Martin's hometown of Atlanta—they moved from Montgomery, Alabama, to Atlanta in 1960—into a branch of the Student Nonviolent Coordinating Committee (SNCC). This group was formed to give younger African Americans a greater role in the civil rights movement, and the students responded by volunteering for the Freedom Riders. The Freedom Riders challenged segregation in bus terminals in the South, and they were often met with violence. Coretta and Martin led a training program, teaching students how to protest nonviolently.

The Shirelles perform at a Freedom Concert in Birmingham, Alabama. Coretta Scott King organized concerts to raise money for the civil rights movement.

Coretta used her singing talents to raise money for the movement. She hosted "Freedom Concerts" in the late 1950s. Despite admission being modest, the concerts raised more than $50,000, which was donated to the Southern Christian Leadership Conference (SCLC). Martin was the first president of the SCLC.

Coretta's efforts grew more and more noticed throughout the world. She came to be known as a supporter not only of black rights but of equal rights for *everybody*. Coretta was invited to the Women's Strike for Peace in Geneva, Switzerland, in 1962. While Coretta often was seen accompanying Martin, she was gaining her own reputation as a mover and a shaker in the civil rights movement.

Coretta Scott King and the Center for Nonviolent Social Change

Violent Backlash

Meanwhile, violence against blacks and their supporters only seemed to worsen. Police assaulted children marching in the Children's Crusade in Birmingham, Alabama, on May 3, 1963, with vicious dogs, tear gas, and high-pressure fire hoses. The children, practicing nonviolence, sang and marched while they were bitten, knocked down, and arrested. In September 1963, a bomb went off in a Birmingham church and four girls were killed. President John F. Kennedy, who had proposed a bill to grant equal rights to all races, was assassinated that November.

Martin Luther King Jr. remained the face of the movement. He gave his famous "I Have a Dream" speech in August 1963. Coretta sat behind him as he said, "I have a dream that my four little children will one day live in a nation where they will not be judged by the color of their skin but by the content of their character." She stood next to him the following year when he was awarded the Nobel Peace Prize.

Martin Luther King Jr. was joined by Coretta Scott King when he accepted the Nobel Peace Prize in Norway on December 10, 1964.

Years of hard work started to pay off in real civil rights progress. After Kennedy's assassination, Lyndon B. Johnson was sworn in as president. He pushed through the Civil Rights Act of 1964, which stated:

> All persons shall be entitled to the full and equal enjoyment of the goods, services, facilities, and privileges, advantages, and accommodations of any place of public accommodation, as defined in this section, without discrimination or segregation on the ground of race, color, religion, or national origin.

The act also took a step toward protecting the right to vote for all Americans, but it wasn't quite strong enough. Blacks were still held back by Jim Crow laws and by de facto segregation. De facto segregation occurs as the result of the preferences of a large number of people even though it's not officially in place by law. Jim Crow laws were state and local laws that enforced segregation in the South. In order to get black voices heard, the Kings spent time focusing on the Voting Rights Act of 1965, which removed voting registration requirements, such as literacy tests and poll taxes, that made it difficult for minorities and the poor to register to vote.

Martin Luther King Jr. had expanded his protests to target the reasons for the poverty in which so many blacks lived. He also protested the war in Vietnam. He said, in an April 4, 1967, speech titled "Beyond Vietnam," that the war was diverting resources from the war on poverty and that it was "an enemy of the poor."

> Perhaps a more tragic recognition of reality took place when it became clear to me the war was doing far more than devastating the hopes of the poor at home … We were taking the black young men who had been

Coretta Scott King and the Center for Nonviolent Social Change

Coretta Scott King (*right*) demonstrated against nuclear weapons as a member of the Women's Strike for Peace.

crippled by our society and sending them eight thousand miles away to guarantee liberties in Southeast Asia which they had not found in southwest Georgia and East Harlem.

Foreseeing His Death

One year to the day later, in the prime of his life, violence stopped Martin from preaching his message of nonviolence. In Memphis, Tennessee, after organizing a protest in support of striking sanitation workers, he was assassinated. Coretta recalled in *My Life with Martin Luther King Jr.* that Martin expected his life might end in such a way. He told her, "You know, I probably won't live a long life, but if I die, I don't want you to grieve for me. You go on and live a normal life … If anything happens to me, you must be prepared to continue."

And so, Coretta continued. She saw the importance of continuing to spread the message of nonviolence. On the day before Martin's funeral, she delivered a speech in Memphis prior to the postponed march he had promised to lead. She spoke at that time of her duty to carry forward his message, saying: "And those of you who believe in what Martin Luther King Jr. stood for, I would challenge you today to see that his spirit never dies and that we will go forward from this experience, which to me represents the Crucifixion, on toward the resurrection and the redemption of the spirit." At the end of her speech, Coretta referenced her husband's death in support for the crusade for change through nonviolence.

> How many men must die before we can really have a free and true and peaceful society? How long will it take? If we can catch the spirit and the true meaning of this experience, I believe that this nation can be transformed into a society of love, of justice, peace, and brotherhood where all men can really be brothers.

Coretta Scott King led a March in Memphis, Tennessee, five days after her husband was assassinated.

Three weeks after her husband was killed, she took his place in giving a speech in New York's Central Park opposing the Vietnam War. She told the audience she drew strength from them: "I come to you in my grief only because you keep alive the work and dreams for which my husband gave his life. My husband arrived somewhere to his strength and

Coretta Scott King and the Center for Nonviolent Social Change

Watching History Being Made

Coretta Scott King has been recognized by world leaders for her efforts in the nonviolent movement. Another protest in which Coretta became heavily involved was against apartheid in South Africa. Apartheid was a system of rigid segregation. Under apartheid, non-white South Africans could not live in the same areas or use the same facilities as their white counterparts. Non-whites were also required to carry documents allowing them to be in "restricted" areas. Only whites could participate in the national government.

Coretta and her children protested at the South African Embassy in Washington, DC, in 1985 and were arrested. Only ten years later, Coretta joined Nelson Mandela in Johannesburg as he was sworn in as the president of South Africa.

President Bill Clinton also acknowledged Coretta's efforts toward nonviolence. He invited her to witness the handshake between Israeli prime minister Yitzhak Rabin and Palestine Liberation Organization (PLO) chairman Yassir Arafat at the signing of the Middle East Peace Accords in 1993. This marked the first face-to-face agreement between the government of Israel and the PLO.

Coretta Scott King (*right*) presented Nelson Mandela with the International Freedom Award in June 1990 in Atlanta.

inspiration from the love of all people who shared his dream, that I too now come hoping you might strengthen me for the lonely road ahead."

Coretta carried on in Martin's place, showing up for his appointments at many speaking engagements. She supported the launching of the Poor People's Campaign in Memphis and a strike of hospital workers in Charleston, South Carolina, among other events.

Coretta Scott King was vocal about equality during an appearance on *Face the Nation* in September 1969.

Coretta was twice on the cover of *Life* magazine. The first time was on April 8, 1968, four days after Martin was killed. She is shown wearing black and described in the article as

Coretta Scott King and the Center for Nonviolent Social Change

"the widow, veiled and beautiful in grief." The second time was September 12, 1969. By then, Coretta had become a staunch activist in her own right, but she was still recognizable because of her marriage to Martin. However, in every speech she made and in every action she undertook, it became clear that she would not simply be telling people what her husband did in the past: she would be picking up right where he left off.

Finding New Purpose

Shortly after her husband's death, Coretta remembered asking herself: "What is it that I'm supposed to do, now that Martin is no longer here?" She developed a vision for a way to permanently honor her husband's message and legacy in the Martin Luther King, Jr. Center for Nonviolent Social Change—the King Center, for short. She envisioned the King Center as "no dead monument, but a living memorial filled with all the vitality that was his, a center of human endeavor, committed to the causes for which he lived and died."

Since being established in 1968, the King Center has become, in words posted on its website, a "global destination, resource center and community institution" that attracts more than a million visitors each year. The King Center is located in Atlanta, Georgia, on a 23-acre (9.3-hectare) national historic site. Martin's birthplace and Ebenezer Baptist Church, where he and his father were both preachers, are part of the King Center's grounds. Martin and Coretta are both buried there.

As the founder, Coretta spread her late husband's message by providing programs throughout the country and the world that trained tens of thousands of people in Martin's philosophy and methods. She organized a way for educational programs to be offered at schools while hosting exhibits, conferences, and immersive training workshops onsite. The goal of these lessons is to make the messages of freedom, justice, and peace part of daily learning for children around the world.

An expansive reflecting pool surrounds the tombs of Coretta Scott King and Martin Luther King Jr. at the Center for Nonviolent Social Change.

Coretta also arranged for events to be hosted at the King Center and other locations. These include everything from camps for teenagers learning to be leaders to speeches from supporters of the nonviolent movement. Every year since 1986, a Commemorative Service has been held on Martin Luther King Jr. Day. A Martin Luther King Jr. Nonviolence Peace Prize is awarded. In the past, the prize has been given to President Jimmy Carter, Rosa Parks, Harry Belafonte, Archbishop Desmond Tutu, and Jesse Jackson, among others.

In recent years, the King Center has embraced technology. A Twitter thread called Nonviolence365 promotes discussion about how to choose a nonviolent lifestyle every day. Often, statements Martin made are shared among Twitter followers. An initiative promoting nonviolence, particularly on Martin Luther King Jr. Day, called "No Shots Fired" offers the option to change social media profiles to share this message.

Under way in 2016 was the development of a curriculum describing Martin's life, accomplishments, and nonviolent teachings for kindergarteners through twelfth graders.

On the King Center's website, thekingcenter.org, there are nearly one million documents that visitors can sift through to

Coretta Scott King and the Center for Nonviolent Social Change

help them understand Martin Luther King Jr.—the person, the activist, the preacher, and the father. Among them are letters, compositions, speeches, telegrams, scribbled notes, patient admonitions, and urgent pleas. Some of the categories of documents include: Letters from Children, Integration of Schools, Photos, Notable **Sermons**, and Global Vision.

The King Center was one outlet Coretta used to promote the work of her husband and to pass on his message. In adition, she thought he should be honored. Coretta was the one to champion the cause of having Martin's birthday recognized as a national holiday. She even testified before a House of Representatives subcommittee because Congress would need to pass a bill in order to have the day recognized. She said, "We strongly feel the nation is in support of this. It would say for many people that the American creed that all people are created equal is important."

Annual Reminder

President Ronald Reagan signed the bill creating the federal holiday on November 2, 1983, and its observation began three years later. In his remarks on the signing, the president said:

Now our nation has decided to honor
Dr. Martin Luther King Jr. by setting aside a
day each year to remember him and the just
cause he stood for. We've made historic strides
since Rosa Parks refused to go to the back of
the bus. As a democratic people, we can take
pride in the knowledge that we Americans
recognized a grave **injustice** and took action to
correct it. And we should remember that in far
too many countries, people like Dr. King never
have the opportunity to speak out at all. But
traces of bigotry still mar America. So, each year
on Martin Luther King Day, let us not only
recall Dr. King, but rededicate ourselves to the
Commandments he believed in and sought to
live every day.

While Coretta may appear to have devoted her life to
Martin's work even after his passing, that is certainly not the
whole story. Coretta traveled across the world to carry the
message of nonviolence. She visited Africa, Latin America,
Europe, and Asia. On one trip, she visited New York City,
London, Oslo, Stockholm, Copenhagen, and Paris.

She became active in fighting for women's rights as well,
serving as a Women's Strike for Peace delegate. She continued
giving speeches about justice, sometimes at rallies attended by
thousands of people.

Coretta also was skilled at bringing people together—
from individuals to giant organizations. As co-chair of both
the National Committee for Full Employment and the Full
Employment Action Council, Coretta created a **coalition**
of more than one hundred religious, labor, business, civil,
and women's rights organizations in 1974. She saw in these
organizations a similar dedication to having a nation that
offered equal economic opportunity, and she thought it

Coretta Scott King and the Center for
Nonviolent Social Change

made sense for everyone to work together. Then, in 1983, she helped eight hundred human rights organizations come together to form the Coalition of Conscience. The Coalition of Conscience sponsored the twentieth and twenty-fifth anniversary Marches on Washington.

Those close to Coretta knew how important her mission was to her. Coretta died at age seventy-eight on January 30, 2006. The poet Maya Angelou gave the eulogy at her funeral and remembered Coretta's commitment to the cause for which she worked for her entire adult life. Angelou recalled phone calls often shared between the two of them and told those gathering in mourning: "Many times on those late after evenings she would say to me, 'Sister, it shouldn't be an "either-or," should it? Peace and justice should belong to all people, everywhere, all the time. Isn't that right?' And I said then and I say now, 'Coretta Scott King, you're absolutely right. I do believe that peace and justice should belong to every person, everywhere, all the time.'"

Coretta Scott King's name may be best remembered because of the man she married. However, she was dedicated to doing everything she could to create a world that accepted everyone and offered everyone the same opportunities. Her husband asked her to continue on, and Coretta truly listened.

CHAPTER THREE

Married to the Movement

C oretta Scott King faced an uphill battle after Martin's death. She still had four young children to raise and protect. Having been such a visible part of the civil rights movement, death threats and intimidation were regular occurrences. But the nonviolent message was one she wished to continue preaching. The cause of equality had always been dear to Coretta's heart. In an interview with the Academy of Achievement, which honored her in 1997, she said:

> "When we decided to get married, it was like marrying the man that I loved, but ... as we were thrust into the forefront of the cause, it was my cause too from the very beginning because I had been an activist in college and was involved in the peace movement and the civil human rights struggle back then at Antioch College.

Coretta Scott King and the Center for Nonviolent Social Change

And so I married not only the man I loved, but I married the cause as well. I could not have continued after he was no [longer] here if I hadn't had that kind of commitment.

So here was Coretta, widowed at a young age and with the nation's eyes on her every move. She did not mourn her husband's death alone. The black community and supporters of the civil rights movement—particularly those for nonviolent social change—were devastated to see their leader gone. But other responses to Martin Luther King Jr.'s death show that some of the people in the United States were not sympathetic to the loss of Martin.

Coretta Scott King balanced her work as an activist with time spent as a mother. She and Martin were the parents of four children.

Sometimes responses were seen in the media. Cartoonist Morrie Turner created a cartoon character named Luther, a nine-year-old black boy, shortly after Martin's assassination. A cartoon he drew shows five children preaching power for each of their individual races, making fists and saying, "Yellow Power! Black Power! Brown Power! Red Power!" Luther steps in to say, "Hey! You guys are all going off in different directions! What we really need around here is Rainbow Power!"

Extolling and Trolling

Some of the responses to Martin's death were more private. Coretta received letters in the mail offering **condolences** for her loss. Many of these came from young children, such as the one from Maria Diaz that read: "Dear Mrs. King, I hope you are feeling better. I am sorry that Mr. King died. He was a very nice man. He tried to teach other people. Everybody loved him. And I loved him to [*sic*]. I heard he was shot last night. Love always, Maria."

Other letters had a nasty tone. A person sent a message from San Diego, California, writing that he or she saw Coretta at the funeral "plotting more riots to carry on the Black Kings' program." As she had to many times, Coretta was forced to deal with the mean-spirited words from people who did not support the Kings' mission.

None of these responses turned her away from her goal. She wanted freedom for her people, and she wanted it to be accomplished through nonviolent means.

However, blacks across the country responded to Martin's assassination with anger and frustration. President Lyndon B. Johnson tried to prevent a backlash, going on national television to ask "every citizen to reject the blind violence that has struck Dr. King, who lived by nonviolence … It is only by joining together and only by working together that we can continue to move toward equality and fulfillment for all people." But many people didn't listen.

Rioting took place in at least 125 cities. This time came to be known as the Holy Week Uprising as some of the violence lasted until Easter Sunday. Windows were broken, **looting** was widespread, and buildings were set on fire. The largest riots were in Washington, DC, where the crowd consisted of about 20,000 people. President Johnson called for 13,600 federal troops and 1,750 National Guard troops to help control the crowds. In the four days following Martin's

Coretta Scott King and the Center for
Nonviolent Social Change

Following the assassination of Martin Luther King Jr., rioting took place in Chicago and many other cities across the country, causing millions of dollars in damages and about forty deaths.

death, 1,200 buildings had been burned, and damages reached $27 million. And that was just in the nation's capital. Large riots also took place in Chicago, Baltimore, Boston, Newark, Detroit, and Kansas City. In total, about 40 people were killed in the riots. Even though Martin had preached nonviolence, not all the blacks he was speaking for could restrain themselves in the face of such injustice.

Support for Violence Grows

African Americans had been tested for a long time. For that reason, some blacks thought violence was the way to bring about change. For all the followers Martin and Coretta had for the nonviolent movement, there were many people who were skeptical it would ever work.

James Meredith was wounded by a sniper's bullet during his March against Fear in 1966. Meredith recovered and joined others who had taken up the march.

Even those who started off supporting the nonviolent movement sometimes wavered. They were frustrated by the slow results. Following the shooting of James Meredith during the March against Fear from Memphis, Tennessee, to Jackson, Mississippi, in 1966, Martin remembered overhearing fellow marchers questioning their mission. In his autobiography, he wrote:

> As we made our trek down that meandering highway amid sweltering heat there was much talk and many questions. "I'm not for that non-violence stuff anymore," shouted one of

Coretta Scott King and the Center for Nonviolent Social Change

the young activists. "If one of these damn white Mississippi crackers touches me, I'm gonna knock the hell out of him," shouted another.

Still other people never even considered nonviolence or marching as a good way to go about seeking change. They wanted progress to come faster, and they thought a different approach was best. Two other groups had a significant presence in the movement at this time.

The Black Panther Party for Self-Defense formed in 1966. Members believed blacks should be arming themselves and preparing to fight against whites. They acted in the name of "self-defense," particularly against police brutality, white mobs, and the Ku Klux Klan. In addition to this mind-set, the Black Panthers also believed in supporting minority groups through community-based programs. For example, they provided free breakfasts to children in **impoverished** areas and sought to establish medical clinics and schools. The language the Black Panthers used to mobilize their supporters was strong, stating: "Your enemy, right now, is the white racist pigs who support this corrupt system."

Response to Hate

The Black Panthers were formed in Oakland, California, partially in response to the actions of the Los Angeles Police Department. Between 1962 and 1964, sixty-five black people were killed by the LAPD, and twenty-seven of them were shot in the back, defenseless. Similar experiences across the country led to a widespread movement. There were Black Panther headquarters set up in sixty-eight cities. They published a newspaper called *The Black Panther: Black Community News Service* that was read by about 150,000 people. Articles were written about the frustration of blacks. One stated "Racism in White America lies on this country like a heavy stench. It is oppressive; it is stifling. It is this very

Opposition to MLK Day

Coretta Scott King fought for fifteen years to get the United States to establish a national holiday in honor of her late husband. It is held on the third Monday in January. In a story she wrote for the King Center website, she said:

> The Martin Luther King Jr. Holiday celebrates the life and legacy of a man who brought hope and healing to America … On this holiday, we commemorate the universal, unconditional love, forgiveness and nonviolence that empowered his revolutionary spirit.

Not everyone agreed that a federal holiday was proper, although some opponents eventually came around. Senator John McCain, a Republican from Arizona, said he originally "thought that it was not necessary to have another federal holiday, that it cost too much money, that other presidents were not recognized." But he later changed his mind, and said in front of the Southern Christian Leadership Conference:

> I was wrong and eventually realized that, in time to give full support for a state holiday in Arizona. We can all be a little late sometimes in doing the right thing, and Dr. King understood this about his fellow Americans.

Jesse Helms, a senator from North Carolina, led a sixteen-day **filibuster** in an attempt to prevent the bill to recognize Martin Luther King Jr. Day from being

Coretta Scott King and the Center for Nonviolent Change

President Ronald Reagan was joined by Coretta Scott King (*right*) when he signed a proclamation to recognize Martin Luther King Jr.'s birthday as a national holiday.

passed. He believed Martin Luther King Jr. associated with communists, and wrote in his memoir:

> Dr. King was a masterful orator. His initial commitment to nonviolence was laudable—but Dr. King was not always careful about his associates or his associations.

same disease that added two more Blacks to its long death list—Bobby Hutton and Dr. King."

The newspaper also included **propaganda** to encourage blacks to support the militant movement. In one such piece of propaganda, a white family is shown holding guns, and the caption read: "White citizens are arming themselves all over the country and organizing their communities not for self-defense, but for the outright slaughter of innocent black citizens." Reading words like this served to mobilize many in the black community who came to support the Black Panther cause.

Black Power

The Nation of Islam was also in opposition to the Kings' approach to solving racial inequality. It was notably led by Malcolm X. This group supported a total black separation from the whites in the country, specifically **economically**. In a famous speech, Malcolm X said:

> All of us have suffered here, in this country, political oppression at the hands of the white man, economic exploitation at the hands of the white man, and social **degradation** at the hands of the white man …
>
> We want freedom now, but we're not going to get it saying "We Shall Overcome." We've got to fight until we overcome.
>
> The economic philosophy of black nationalism is pure and simple. It only means that we should control the economy of our community. Why should white people be running all the stores in our community? Why should white people be running the banks of our community? Why should the economy of our community be in the hands of the white man? Why? If a black man can't move his store into a

Coretta Scott King and the Center for Nonviolent Social Change

The Black Panthers opposed the Kings' view of nonviolence, as they preached a message of self-defense to stop the attacks against minorities.

white community, you tell me why a white man should move his store into a black community.

Members of the Black Panthers and the Nation of Islam were sick of being treated as second-class citizens in just the same way the Kings were—they just had different tactics in mind to **remedy** the discrimination. By 1967, under the slogan of "Black Power," many people in the black community believed that no real change would happen without violence. The Kings' message was being **undermined**.

The debate over how to approach the fight for freedom was so popular that a fiction book was written about it. *The Rock and the River* is the story of two brothers growing up during the civil rights era, one following his father's footsteps in nonviolence and the other joining the Black Panthers.

Aside from the Black Panthers and the Nation of Islam, others were suspicious of or against the efforts of Coretta following her husband's death. Martin had been the head of the Southern Christian Leadership Conference. The SCLC was skeptical of Coretta's plan to create the King Center. The leadership in place after Martin's death feared that the money Coretta would be raising to form the King Center would take away from the funds the SCLC needed.

In addition to the building of the King Center, Coretta made it her mission to have her late husband's birthday recognized as a national holiday. It may seem like an obvious choice now to honor Martin Luther King Jr., but many disagreed with it at the time. In order to have a day called a "national holiday," Congress must vote to do so. In 1983, members of the House of Representatives approved the holiday by a vote of 338 to 90. Members of the Senate approved the holiday by a vote of 78 to 22. That means 112 members of Congress did not want Martin Luther King Jr.'s birthday to be celebrated across the country.

Since more people supported than opposed the holiday, President Ronald Reagan signed the Congressional bill into law in 1983, but it was not observed nationally until 1986. Some states resisted celebrating the day as a holiday. In fact, it wasn't until 2000 that all fifty states officially observed Martin Luther King Jr. Day. Even today, some states honor others along with Martin Luther King Jr. In Alabama, Mississippi, and Arkansas, people also celebrate Confederate general Robert E. Lee's birthday (Martin Luther King Jr. was born January 15, and Robert E. Lee on January 19). In Idaho, the day is considered Martin Luther King Jr. Idaho Human Rights Day. In New Hampshire, the day is called Martin Luther King Jr. Civil Rights Day.

Coretta Scott King and the Center for
Nonviolent Social Change

Denver, Colorado, hosts the largest Martin Luther King Day Parade in the country. Here marchers fill Colfax Avenue in 2010.

Married to the Movement

CHAPTER
FOUR

Expanding the Fight

Coretta Scott King will be most remembered for her contributions to the civil rights movement that sought equality for black Americans. Since she and her husband committed themselves to this cause, opportunities for blacks have expanded. There are no longer any laws in place that keep blacks separate from whites in the United States. Blacks have access to and use of public accommodations, the right to vote, and fair employment and housing opportunities. Much of the progress was achieved through nonviolent means, the way the Kings outlined.

Coretta's efforts, however, did not end with the civil rights movement. She created a legacy independent of her husband by supporting other causes. Martin Luther King Jr. was alive when race seemed to be the primary means of discrimination. But skin color is far from the only reason for which people are

Coretta Scott King and the Center for
Nonviolent Social Change

treated wrong. Coretta shifted her energy to also help fight for other **disenfranchised** groups.

Just four days after Martin's death, Coretta preached to the women. In her famous speech renouncing the Vietnam War, Coretta finished by saying:

> I would now like to address myself to the women. The woman power of this nation can be the power which makes us whole and heals the rotten community, now so shattered by war and poverty and racism. I have great faith in the power of women who will dedicate themselves whole-heartedly to the task of remaking our society. I believe that the women of this nation and of the world are the best and last hope for a world of peace and brotherhood.

Martin Focused on Race

Gender equality was not a priority of Martin's. In fact, through his actions, he even indicated that he felt men were better for certain roles. Gwendolyn Simmons, an activist who was associated with the nonviolent cause, wrote about Martin's decisions to exclude women in an essay called "Martin Luther King Jr. Revisited: A Black Power Feminist Pays Homage to the King." She argues that Martin's **sexism** was obvious because he refused to promote prominent activist Ella Baker into a permanent leadership role with the Southern Christian Leadership Conference.

> The civil rights movement was hardly a model of female inclusion in the area of leadership. **Patriarchy** plagued the black freedom struggle on all sides … All men had difficulty seeing

Coretta Scott King, John Lewis, and Reverend Jesse Jackson attended a march on the fortieth anniversary of her husband's "I Have a Dream" speech.

women in leadership roles. King's inability to see movement women as his peers and even mentors prevented him from forging strong connections with radical black women who could have been his greatest allies in the struggle he was about to launch against economic oppression.

Coretta Scott King and the Center for Nonviolent Social Change

In her essay, Simmons ultimately gave Martin the benefit of the doubt. She thinks that had Martin lived longer he may have seen the full value of women to the civil rights movement. Coretta, being a woman herself, did not waste time encouraging women to be a part of the fight. She famously said: "Women, if the soul of the nation is to be saved, I believe that you must become its soul."

President of Ireland Mary Robinson (*left*) and American poet Maya Angelou (*center*) join Coretta Scott King at the 1996 International Women's Forum.

One way in which Coretta stood by her cause was by attending the Soviet-American Women's Summit in 1990, which called for "the full and effective participation of women at every level of decision-making to ensure the comprehensive vision and democratic action needed to address the urgent challenges of our times." The nature of the gathering also was in line with Coretta's way of thinking. The Soviet Union and United States of America were engaged in the Cold War for forty-five years prior to the meeting. This summit marked groups coming together for the greater good.

Standing Up for Gays

After Martin's death, Coretta publicly supported the gay rights movement. Due to Martin's early death, people were left to guess his interpretation on homosexuality and the gay rights movement. One indication that Martin may have been less than supportive came in 1958. When he was writing an advice column for *Ebony* magazine, he received a message from a boy who wrote: "My problem is different from the ones most people have. I am a boy, but I feel about boys the way I ought to feel about girls. I don't want my parents to know about me. What can I do? Is there any place where I can go for help?" Martin spoke of the boy's "problem" as something "that has been culturally acquired." He finished by responding that the boy should visit a psychiatrist but was already on "the right road toward a solution, since you honestly recognize the problem and have a desire to solve it." Martin never took a public stand regarding homosexuality.

Coretta believed Martin would have supported gay rights, saying at a conference that:

> My husband, Martin Luther King Jr., once said, "We are all tied together in a single garment of destiny … an inescapable network of mutuality … I can never be what I ought to be until you are allowed to be what you ought to be." Therefore, I appeal to everyone who believes in Martin Luther King Jr.'s dream to make room at the table of brotherhood and sisterhood for lesbian and gay people.

Supporters of equal rights for gay people state that sexuality is **innate** to each person, meaning a person is born liking males or females. These supporters believe gay people should have the same rights as straight people. They also believe two people should be allowed to marry one another no matter what their gender. Opponents say that gay people choose to be gay and could choose to change. They also claim that allowing gays to wed will undermine marriage and be bad for children. The gay rights movement has recently gained momentum. Some have even called it the "new civil rights."

Coretta Scott King and the Center for Nonviolent Social Change

The Black Lives Matter movement began as a response to police shootings of blacks, mostly men.

Black Lives Matter

The fight for equal treatment appears to be coming full circle with the Black Lives Matter movement, which has thirty chapters throughout the United States. Black Lives Matter calls itself "a chapter-based national organization working for the validity of Black life." The organization was formed as a reaction to a perception that blacks were being mistreated by the state and because of police brutality against the black community.

The Black Lives Matter movement is asking American society to reconsider how it values black lives. Thousands of Americans are furthering the mission of the Kings through nonviolence. One of the visions of Black Lives Matter speaks to the "Beloved Community" that Martin envisioned, saying, "We are committed to collectively, lovingly and courageously working vigorously for freedom and justice for Black people and, by extension, all people. As we forge our path, we intentionally build and nurture a beloved community that is bonded together through a beautiful struggle that is restorative, not depleting."

Expanding the Fight 47

The gay rights movement borrowed a page from the civil rights movement in utilizing peaceful marches to fight for equality.

Martin may not have been directly involved with this movement, but Coretta and other members of their family have taken a stand. Not all the Kings are in agreement. Martin and Coretta's youngest daughter, Bernice, said at a conference in New Zealand, "I know deep down in my sanctified soul that [Martin] did not take a bullet for same-sex unions." Bernice shifted her stance some since that comment. In a speech about building unity, she preached about coming across all boundaries, including "heterosexual or homosexual."

Of all the Kings, Coretta didn't seem to need time to think about where she stood. Throughout the struggles gay Americans had in their fight for equal rights, Coretta made clear her support for the lesbian, gay, bisexual, and transgender

Coretta Scott King and the Center for Nonviolent Social Change

(LGBT) community. In 1983, Coretta pledged her support for the Gay and Civil Rights Act before Congress. She also invited Audre Lorde, a black lesbian, to speak at the twentieth anniversary of the 1963 March on Washington, even though this decision was not popular among all attending. Coretta later spoke at a Human Rights Campaign Fund dinner to express her solidarity with the LGBT movement. She famously compared the struggles of blacks and gay people by saying:

> Homophobia is like racism and anti-Semitism and other forms of bigotry in that it seeks to dehumanize a large group of people, to deny their humanity, their dignity and personhood.

She wasn't afraid to stand up to the nation's leaders. In 1993, she held a press conference urging President Bill Clinton to stop banning gay people from serving openly in the US military. In 2004, President George W. Bush pledged his support for a constitutional amendment that defined marriage as "a union of a man and a woman." Coretta publicly opposed his stance in a speech given to college students in 2004 when she said, "Gay and lesbian people have families, and their families should have legal protection, whether by marriage or civil union. A constitutional amendment banning same-sex marriage is a form of gay bashing and it would do nothing to protect traditional marriages."

Coretta and proponents of gay rights have had many victories in recent years. From 2003 to 2015, thirty-eight of the United States legalized gay marriage to some extent. Then, in June 2015, the United States Supreme Court ruled in *Obergefell v. Hodges* that states were not allowed to ban same-sex marriage. In the decision, Justice Anthony Kennedy wrote: "The right to marry is a fundamental right inherent in the liberty of the person, and under the Due Process and Equal Protection Clauses of the Fourteenth Amendment couples of the same sex may not be deprived of that right and that liberty. Same-sex couples may exercise the fundamental right to marry." And with that, another group that once was discriminated against was given its rights.

Nonviolence Helped Many Causes

The causes Coretta supported in the years after Martin's death were clearly close to her heart. However, the lasting impact of the nonviolent movement has affected dozens of causes with which she had no direct involvement at all. Her commitment to spreading Martin's philosophy and the benefits of nonviolence has helped many groups make their stand.

People opposed to the Vietnam War also used nonviolent demonstrations to spread their message of peace.

In one of her very first speeches after Martin's passing, Coretta denounced the Vietnam War. Many other Americans also were opposed. They took a page from the book of nonviolent protest to get their point across. A famous photograph taken at the time shows a seventeen-year-old,

Coretta Scott King and the Center for Nonviolent Social Change

Coretta Scott King's funeral was widely attended. Mourners also paid their respects when she became the first woman and black person to lie in honor in Georgia's capitol.

Jan Rose Kasmir, holding a flower while guns and bayonets are being pointed at her. Activists wanted to show their opposition to America's involvement in the Vietnam War, but they would not use violence to make their voices heard.

In more recent years, a movement that came to include thousands of people in protest was called Occupy Wall Street. Protesters wanted to show how upset they were that the very richest Americans and their organizations have so much power over the American government. They also were angry about the huge **disparity**—or gap—in wealth between the rich and the middle and poor classes. These protesters used slogans, as had people involved in the civil rights movement, that became their battle cry. The most well-known slogan was "We are the 99 percent," which spoke to the protesters' frustration about the top 1 percent of the richest Americans getting richer while everyone else did not have the same opportunities. This movement spread to eighty-two countries that had similar wage disparities.

Coretta Scott King and Martin Luther King Jr. were visionaries for the way to achieve social change. And while Martin may still be the face of the civil rights movement, Coretta's contributions were extensive and important as well. She ultimately helped give a voice to the women supporting that cause and many others.

Through her work with the King Center, Coretta made certain that generations of children and adults will understand the work of her husband and the philosophy of nonviolence. By pushing for her husband's birthday to be celebrated as a national holiday, Coretta ensured the whole nation would spend at least one day each year thinking about the fight for racial equality that had nothing to do with weapons or fists.

Coretta Scott King and the Center for
Nonviolent Social Change

Chronology

Dates in green pertain to events discussed in this volume.

1863 The Emancipation Proclamation is issued by President Abraham Lincoln

1865 The Thirteenth Amendment, abolishing slavery, is passed in the US House of Representatives. The amendment was passed by the Senate in 1864.

1868 The Fourteenth Amendment, guaranteeing equal rights under the law, is passed.

1870 The Fifteenth Amendment, prohibiting governments from denying male citizens the right to vote based on their race, is passed.

1883 The Supreme Court strikes down the Civil Rights Act of 1875, which guaranteed equal rights to all African Americans in transportation, restaurants or inns, theaters, and on juries.

1896 *Plessy v. Ferguson*, establishing the precedent of "separate but equal," is handed down by the Supreme Court of the United States.

1909 The National Association for the Advancement of Colored People (NAACP) is established.

1927 Coretta Scott is born in Marion, Alabama, on April 27.

1935 Thurgood Marshall and Charles Hamilton Houston successfully sue the University of Maryland, arguing for Donald Murray's admission to the institution's law school in *Murray v. Pearson*.

1941 President Franklin D. Roosevelt bans discrimination against minorities in the granting of defense contracts.

1945 Coretta Scott enrolls in Antioch College in Yellow Springs, Ohio.

1947 Jackie Robinson breaks the color barrier, becoming the first African American to play in Major League Baseball.

1953 Coretta Scott marries Martin Luther King Jr. on June 18.

1954 Thurgood Marshall aze NAACP win the case of *Brown v. Board of Education of Topeka*, which overturns *Plessy v. Ferguson* and the "separate but equal" doctrine of segregation in the United States.

1955 Rosa Parks refuses to give up her seat to a white person on a bus in Montgomery, Alabama. Her arrest sparks a bus boycott that leads to buses being desegregated in that city. Martin Luther King Jr. helps organize the boycott.

1956 A bomb is thrown at the Kings' house when Coretta is home with her youngest daughter.

1957 Federal troops are called in to protect nine African American students in Little Rock, Arkansas, who are trying to attend all-white Central High School.

1958 Coretta Scott King and Martin Luther King Jr. spend a month in India learning about Gandhi and his nonviolent practices.

1961 President John F. Kennedy issues an executive order prohibiting discrimination in federal hiring on the basis of race, religion, or national origin. The order establishes the President's Committee on Equal Employment Opportunity.

1961 Congress on Racial Equality organizes Freedom Rides throughout the South, and the riders suffer beatings from mobs in many cities.

1963 The March on Washington attracts a quarter of a million people, who listen to Martin Luther King Jr.'s "I Have a Dream" speech.

1964 President Lyndon B. Johnson signs the Civil Rights Act of 1964. It prohibits discrimination of all kinds.

1965 When an effort to register black voters is met with resistance in the South, Martin Luther King Jr. and the Southern Christian Leadership Conference organize a march for voting rights in Alabama from Selma to Montgomery. Congress passes the Voting Rights Act, which guarantees to all African Americans the right to vote.

1967 Thurgood Marshall becomes the first African-American Supreme Court justice. He is nominated by Lyndon Johnson after his admirable work as an attorney, circuit judge, and solicitor general.

1968 Martin Luther King Jr. is assassinated in Memphis, Tennessee, on April 4. He is there to support a sanitation workers strike. Coretta Scott King takes her husband's place in speaking against the Vietnam War, and she founds the King Center for Nonviolent Social Change.

1979 Coretta Scott King testifies for the first time seeking recognition of Martin Luther King Jr.'s birthday as a national holiday.

1983 President Ronald Reagan signs a bill commemorating Martin Luther King Jr. Day as a national holiday on November 2.

1998 Coretta Scott King calls on the civil rights community to join the gay rights movement.

2006 Coretta Scott King dies.

Coretta Scott King and the Center for Nonviolent Social Change

Glossary

coalition A combination or alliance of people, factions, or states.

condolences An expression of sympathy for a person who is suffering sorrow, misfortune, or grief.

degradation The act of humiliating or reducing someone to a lower rank; dehumanizing.

disenfranchised Deprived of a right of citizenship or privilege.

disparity A lack of equality, such as a gap in wages or treatment between groups.

economically Regarding one's personal financial resources.

filibuster The use of tactics by a member of a legislature to prevent the adoption of a measure by making a long speech or series of speeches.

inferior Lower in place or position, or lower in quality.

injustice Violation of the rights of others, or unfair treatment under the law.

innate Existing from birth or natural.

looting To steal goods from a business, especially during a riot.

lynch To put to death outside the legal system by hanging or other forms of violence.

patriarchy A social system in which power is held by men.

propaganda Information or principles spread by an organization or movement.

remedy Something that cures or relieves.

sermons Commentaries given by a pastor, minister, or priest during a church service, usually for the purpose of religious instruction.

sexism Attitudes based on traditional stereotypes of gender roles.

theology The study of religion or divinity; a system of religious beliefs.

undermined Weakened by indirect, secret, or underhanded means.

Coretta Scott King and the Center for Nonviolent Social Change

Further Information

Books

Bagley, Edythe Scott. *Desert Rose: The Life and Legacy of Coretta Scott King*. Tuscaloosa, AL: University of Alabama Press, 2012.

King, Coretta Scott. *My Life with Martin Luther King, Jr.* Revised edition. New York: Henry Holt, 1993.

Klingel, Cynthia Fitterer. *Coretta Scott King*. Chanhassen: Child's World, 1999.

Press, Petra. *Coretta Scott King: An Unauthorized Biography*. Chicago: Heinemann Library, 2000.

Terp, Gail. *Nonviolent Resistance in the Civil Rights Movement*. Minneapolis, MN: Core Library, 2016.

Websites

Academy of Achievement: Coretta Scott King Profile

www.achievement.org/autodoc/page/kin1pro-1

Listen to an interview with Coretta as she was recognized by the Academy of Achievement. She discusses her life with Martin and many other important topics.

The Martin Luther King, Jr. Center for Nonviolent Social Change

www.thekingcenter.org

Explore archives from the civil rights movement, learning about the efforts of Martin Luther King Jr. as Coretta preserved them.

***New York Times*: Coretta Scott King Obituary**

www.nytimes.com/2006/01/31/national/31cnd-coretta.html?pagewanted=all&_r=0

Read Coretta's obituary published in the *New York Times*, which honors her life and efforts toward achieving equality.

Coretta Scott King and the Center for
Nonviolent Social Change

Bibliography

Abidor, Mitchell, trans. "Warning to So-Called 'Paper Panthers'" *The Black Panther*, September 28, 1968. Accessed January 29, 2016. http://www.marxists.org/history/usa/workers/black-panthers/1968/paper-panthers.htm.

"About the Black Lives Matter Network." Black Lives Matter. Accessed January 29, 2016. http://blacklivesmatter.com/about.

Amira, Dan. "The Eight Current Members of Congress Who Voted Against Martin Luther King Jr. Day." *Daily Intelligencer*, January 21, 2013. Accessed January 29, 2016. http://nymag.com/daily/intelligencer/2013/01/voted-against-mlk-day-mccain-hatch-grassley-shelby.html.

Angelou, Maya. "Eulogy for Coretta Scott King." Eulogy, New Birth Missionary Baptist Church, Lithonia. February 7, 2006. Accessed January 29, 2016. https://www.youtube.com/watch?v=otGXTryeY6w.

Blake, John. "MLK Was a Republican and Other Myths." CNN. January 18, 2016. Accessed January 29, 2016. http://www.cnn.com/2016/01/15/us/mlk-myths.

Brunner, Borgna, and Elissa Hanney. "Civil Rights Timeline." Infoplease. Accessed January 29, 2016. http://www.infoplease.com/spot/civilrightstimeline1.html.

Harris, Brandon. "The Most Important Legacy of the Black Panthers." *New Yorker*, September 4, 2015. Accessed January 29, 2016. http://www.newyorker.com/culture/culture-desk/the-most-important-legacy-of-the-black-panthers.

"In Praise of the Soviet-American Women's Summit," Congressional Record Cong., E1759 (1990) (testimony of Hon. Claudine Schneider). http://thomas.loc.gov/cgi-bin/query/z?r101:E24MY0-B417:.

"Mexican Americans Fight Racism." *The Black Panther*, May 4, 1968. Accessed January 29, 2016. http://www.itsabouttimebpp.com/BPP_Newspapers/pdf/Vol_II_No1_1968.pdf.

Johnson, Lyndon B. "Statement by LBJ on the Assassination of Martin Luther King, Jr." Speech, April 4, 1968. Accessed January 29, 2016. http://www.pbs.org/wgbh/americanexperience/features/primary-resources/lbj-assassination/?flavour=mobile.

King, Coretta Scott. "10 Commandments on Vietnam." Speech, Central Park, New York, April 27, 1968. Accessed January 29, 2016. http://www.americanrhetoric.com/speeches/corettascottkingvietnamcommandments.htm.

King, Martin Luther Jr. "I've Been to the Mountaintop." Speech, Masonic Temple, Memphis, Tennessee, April 3, 1968. Accessed January 29, 2016. http://www.americanrhetoric.com/speeches/mlkivebeentothemountaintop.htm.

———. "I Have a Dream." Speech, Lincoln Memorial, Washington, DC, August 28, 1963. Accessed January 29, 2016. http://www.americanrhetoric.com/speeches/mlkihaveadream.htm.

Lincoln, Abraham. "Emancipation Proclamation." Speech, January 1, 1863. Accessed January 29, 2016. http://www.archives.gov/exhibits/featured_documents/emancipation_proclamation/transcript.html.

Coretta Scott King and the Center for Nonviolent Social Change

Long, Michael G. "Coretta's Big Dream: Coretta Scott King on Gay Rights." *Huffington Post.* January 31, 2013. Accessed January 29, 2016. http://www.huffingtonpost.com/michael-g-long/coretta-scott-king_b_2592049.html.

Malcolm X. "The Ballot or the Bullet." Speech, Cleveland, April 3, 1964. Accessed January 29, 2016. http://www.edchange.org/multicultural/speeches/malcolm_x_ballot.html.

"Profeminist." *Profeminist.* January 19, 2015. Accessed January 29, 2016. http://profeminist.tumblr.com/post/108616727687/martin-luther-king-jr-in-feminist-perspective.

"Selma to Montgomery March (1965)." Martin Luther King, Jr. and the Global Freedom Struggle. Accessed January 29, 2016. http://kingencyclopedia.stanford.edu/encyclopedia/encyclopedia/enc_selma_to_montgomery_march.

"Social Movements Will Put an End to War as We Know It." Occupy Wall Street. Accessed January 29, 2016. http://occupywallst.org.

Smiley, Tavis. "Civil Rights Activist Coretta Scott King." PBS, January 18, 2013. Accessed January 29, 2016. http://www.pbs.org/wnet/tavissmiley/interviews/civil-rights-activist-coretta-scott-king

"30 Years of Celebrating MLK Day: What's It Mean to You." *The State Journal (Frankfort)*, January 18, 2016. http://www.state-journal.com/opinion/2016/01/18/30-years-of-celebrating-mlk-day-what-s-it-mean-to-you.

Index

Page numbers in **boldface** are illustrations. Entries in **boldface** are glossary terms.

Coretta Scott King and the Center for Nonviolent Social Change

gender equality and,
43–45
marriage, 12, 14
nonviolence and, 5–6, 14,
18, 33–35, 42
speeches, 5–6, 19–20
King Center, 25–27, **26–27**,
36, 40, 52

looting, 32
lynch, 5, 11

Malcolm X, 38–39
March on Washington, 19,
29, **44**, 49
Meredith, James, 34, **34**
Montgomery bus boycott,
15–16, **16**

NAACP, 11–12, **12**, 14–15
Nation of Islam, 38–40
Nobel Peace Prize, 19, **19**

Obergefell v. Hodges, 49–50
Occupy Wall Street, 51–52

Parks, Rosa, 15, 26, 28
patriarchy, 43
propaganda, 38

Reagan, Ronald, 27–28, 37, 40
remedy, 39

SCLC, 18, 36, 40, 43
sermons, 27
sexism, 43
Soviet-American Women's
Summit, 45

theology, 12

undermined, 39, 46

Vietnam War, 20–22, 43,
50–51, **50**
Voting Rights Act, 20

Women's Strike for Peace,
18, **21**, 28

About the Author

JACKIE F. STANMYRE is a social worker and writer. She worked as a newspaper reporter at the *Star-Ledger* of Newark, New Jersey, before beginning a new career in mental health and addictions treatment. As a children's book author, she has written for the Dangerous Drugs, Game-Changing Athletes, and It's My State! series. Jackie lives in New Jersey with her husband and son.